CARRIE UNDERWOOD

Laura La Bella

rosen publishing's
rosen
central

New York

Published in 2008 by The Rosen Publishing Group, Inc.
29 East 21st Street, New York, NY 10010

First Edition

Library of Congress Cataloging-in-Publication Data

La Bella, Laura.
Carrie Underwood / Laura La Bella. — 1st ed.
    p.cm. — (Who's your Idol?)
Includes bibliographical references and index.
ISBN-13: 978-1-4042-1370-8 (library binding)
1. Underwood, Carrie, 1983—Juvenile literature. 2. Singers—United States—Biography—Juvenile literature. I. Title.
ML3930.U53C37 2008
782.421642092—dc22
(B)

        2007039666

Manufactured in the United States of America

Contents

Introduction

When Carrie Underwood stepped on stage to accept the award for Top Female Vocalist at the Academy of Country Music Awards in May 2005, she couldn't help but mention *American Idol*—the wildly popular television show and singing competition—in her acceptance speech. "I would not be here if it were not for *American Idol*," she told the audience as she accepted the award.

It's been a whirlwind of a ride for Carrie Underwood, a small-town girl from Checotah, Oklahoma, who had dreams of becoming a singer. She began her career singing in church as a child and soon was performing in local events and at festivals in and around Oklahoma. These early performances got the attention of a record company that was interested in signing her. Unfortunately, the deal fell apart. But she kept on singing.

One year after winning the *American Idol* crown, Carrie Underwood returns to the Kodak Theatre in Hollywood, California, for the Season 5 finale. She performs her number 1 hit, "Don't Forget to Remember Me."

Underwood went to college to study mass communications and continued to sing at events and in an annual country music show. The auditions for Season Four of *American Idol* were beginning. It was her friends and family who pushed her to try out. As her senior year of college approached, even Underwood thought that this might be her last opportunity to see if she could make it as a singer. When she made it through the first round of auditions and was invited to Hollywood, many people early on were impressed by her innocent charm and pure, pretty voice and thought she would win the competition.

And she did.

Carrie Underwood became the winner of Season Four of *American Idol*. Her rise to fame started soon after she won. Her first single, "Inside Your Heaven," which she sang during the finale of the show, debuted at number 1 on the Billboard Hot 100 and the Canadian Singles charts. Her first album, *Some Hearts*, was the highest-selling country album by a debut artist. It was certified platinum six times, selling more than six million copies, and has since produced four number 1 hits.

Underwood's win at the Academy of Country Music Awards is just one in a number of honors the singer has earned. She has won several other major music awards, including a host of honors from the country music industry. She is the first *American Idol* winner to receive honors at all three of the major music awards shows (the Grammy Awards, the American Music Awards, and the Billboard Music Awards) in the same award-show season. And she's the only *American Idol* champion to win the prestigious Best New Artist award at the Grammys.

Carrie Underwood has become one of the most successful *American Idol* winners to date. Though she has already enjoyed almost unprecedented levels of success, Underwood still stands at the threshold of her musical career. She has only just begun, and she shows no signs of stopping.

A SMALL-TOWN GIRL

Checotah, Oklahoma, is a small town of only 3,800 people. It is located on the southeastern edge of the Great Plains, approximately 70 miles (112.6 kilometers) southeast of Tulsa. It is home to a large number of antiques malls, a Civil War battle site, and a downtown historic district. Checotah claims to be the "Steer Wrestling Capital of the World." But its biggest claim to fame these days just might be that it is the hometown of Carrie Underwood, the 2005 *American Idol* winner.

A Star Is Born

Carrie Underwood was born on March 10, 1983, at the Muskogee Regional Medical Center in Muskogee, Oklahoma. The town, made famous in the song "Okie from Muskogee" by country singing legend

Oklahoma governor Brad Henrey and his wife, Kim, present Underwood with a replica of a road sign that was placed in her hometown of Checotah, Oklahoma.

Merle Haggard, is only a few miles from Checotah, Underwood's hometown.

"I began my life with the best family in the world already waiting for me," Underwood wrote in the biography on her Web site. Underwood is the third and youngest daughter born to Steve and Carole Underwood. Her father worked for thirty years as a paper mill operator for Georgia-Pacific until he retired to raise cattle on their farm. Her mother was a fifth grade English teacher in the Checotah Public School District.

Growing up on the Oklahoma cattle farm, Underwood was surrounded by family, including her two older sisters, Shanna and Stephanie. Shanna is thirteen years older than Carrie, and Stephanie is ten years older. Both sisters followed in their mother's footsteps and became teachers in Oklahoma school districts.

Underwood was especially close with her mom, and her only childhood conflict with her arose during the few instances in which her mother served as the substitute teacher in her class. "I stuck my tongue out behind her back once," Underwood told Velvetrope.com in an interview. "I got told on."

Because her two sisters were so much older than her, Underwood spent a lot of time with her mother, and a strong bond grew between the two. "(My mom) was mainly the person I hung out with," Underwood told *Reader's Digest.* "It might sound a little dorky, but we'd go shopping and to the movies together and have mommy-daughter days all the time."

A tomboy growing up, Underwood would climb trees and play on her family's farm. "I'd jump in hay bales and play with the cows," she said in that same *Reader's Digest* interview. She told *Parade* magazine that she and her friends all had big yards and would climb trees and play in ditches and ponds.

Underwood's family were members of the Free Will Baptist Church in Checotah. Underwood was involved in a number of church activities, from before-school prayer meetings to holiday gatherings for the church's youngest members. "We were

Underwood celebrates at the Academy of Country Music Awards with her mother, Carole. That night, she won awards for Female Vocalist of the Year and Single Record of the Year.

raised in church," she told *Reader's Digest*. "It was your typical all-American family."

An Early Interest in Music

Underwood's parents liked fifties- and sixties-era records, and her two older sisters liked the pop music of the 1980s. "I was exposed to pretty much everything growing up," Underwood told Kidzworld.com. She listened to groups like the Beatles

Among Underwood's musical influences were the Beatles, one of the most commercially successful and critically acclaimed bands of all time. Underwood also listened to rock and pop music from the 1980s.

and Creedence Clearwater Revival. But Underwood favored country music. "To me, it's the most respectable kind of music. It's honest," she told *Parade* magazine. "The people are genuinely talented."

Musical talent didn't run in her family, but Underwood began to show signs of her singing ability at a young age. She started singing in church when she was just three years old. Once she was in school, Underwood frequently sang solo roles in musical plays. Soon she was performing in local community events, at festivals in Oklahoma and neighboring states, and at talent shows for Old Settler's Day and other events. By the time she was in seventh grade, people were taking notice of Underwood's talent, often telling her she had a big voice for such a young girl.

Along with developing her singing voice, Underwood learned how to play the guitar and the piano. But it was singing that she liked most, and she loved to perform. "I pushed my mom to take me to local talent shows," Underwood wrote in the biography on her Web site, www.carrieunderwoodofficial.com. "I never won but usually placed. I was so excited when I won a $25 saving bonds or a trophy. Little did I know that those things would someday lead me down the road I'm on today."

Underwood continued to sing at festivals and perform in school events all during her childhood. Her music teacher even cast her as a Mother Nature figure who sang to animals in a fourth-grade production.

When Underwood was only thirteen years old, her manager tried to get her a recording contract at Capitol Records, a world-famous record label. There were many changes happening at the company at that time, however, and unfortunately, Underwood never got a record contract. While it was disappointing for Underwood, she didn't stop singing.

High School and College Years

Many of Underwood's high school teachers describe her as being sweet, smart, and shy. Underwood was athletic. She was a cheerleader and played softball and basketball in high school. She regularly performed the national anthem at her high school's sporting events and performed in the school talent show.

But it was in the classroom where Underwood really shined. She took her studies very seriously. She was a strong student and excelled at Checotah High School. She worked hard and graduated as the salutatorian—the person with the second-best

Southern *American Idol* Winners

The first six *American Idol* winners have all been from the southern or southwestern United States. Here's a look at where they're from:

Season One	Kelly Clarkson	Fort Worth, Texas
Season Two	Ruben Studdard	Birmingham, Alabama
Season Three	Fantasia Barrino	High Point, North Carolina
Season Four	Carrie Underwood	Checotah, Oklahoma
Season Five	Taylor Hicks	Birmingham, Alabama
Season Six	Jordin Sparks	Phoenix, Arizona

grades—in the Class of 2001. Underwood sported an unusual look at her high school graduation ceremony when she delivered her salutatorian speech. She had a black eye, courtesy of a stray ball that hit her during a softball game.

After high school, Underwood entered her freshman year at Northeastern State University (NSU) in Tahlequah, Oklahoma, a small town located about 55 miles (88.5 km) northeast of Checotah. Underwood decided to study mass communications.

Once she arrived at college, Underwood immediately got involved in school activities, which ranged from producing a student-run television program to writing for the *Northeastern*, the school's student newspaper. As she looked toward her future after college, Underwood imagined a career in broadcast journalism and thought about getting a job at one of the local television stations in Tulsa, the second-largest city in Oklahoma.

Even though Underwood admits that she was shy in college, she became a social presence at NSU. She joined a sorority, which is an all-girls social organization that often holds events to raise money for causes or whose members volunteer in the community. Underwood's sorority is named Sigma Sigma Sigma. She also became a member of the Muscogee Creek Nation of Oklahoma, a group of Native Americans originally from the southeastern United States.

Even though she was so active in clubs and organizations while in college, Underwood was never far from a stage. Her friends always wanted her to sing at events, and she continued to perform at shows. She took part in NSU's Downtown Country Show, where she learned about country music legends like Patsy Cline and the Carter family. She also started to become more comfortable singing in front of a large audience. Underwood even entered beauty pageants. While she didn't win the Miss NSU pageant, despite being selected as the runner-up, she did win the talent competition.

In 2004, Underwood auditioned for *American Idol*. When she made it to the semifinals and finals in Hollywood, she left college to compete on the show. After winning *American Idol*, however, Underwood didn't let the sudden fame go to her head. Instead she returned to NSU to finish her degree. In May 2006, Underwood walked across the stage at the Jack Dobbins Field House and received her diploma. "Picking

After winning *American Idol*, Underwood wanted to accomplish one more thing: she wanted to graduate from college. In this photo, she accepts her diploma from Northeastern State University in May 2006.

up my diploma was very important to me," Underwood told *People* magazine. She graduated magna cum laude (meaning with high honors) with a bachelor of arts degree in mass communications.

Chapter 2

AUDITIONING FOR AMERICAN IDOL

The auditions for Season Four of *American Idol* started in August 2004 and ran until October. Auditions were held in seven American cities: Cleveland, Ohio; Las Vegas, Nevada; New Orleans, Louisiana; Orlando, Florida; San Francisco, California; St. Louis, Missouri; and Washington, D.C.

Season Four featured a change in the rules that allowed even more people to audition. The age limit for contestants was raised to twenty-eight years old. Two contestants benefited from this change: Constantine Maroulis and Bo Bice, who were the oldest of the season's contestants and had the most musical experience. Maroulis and Bice were considered the two "rockers" among the new crop of competitors. They stood out from the other

On the final night of the season, Underwood and fellow finalist Bo Bice arrive together at the Kodak Theatre for the results show.

singers with their long hair; choice of songs, which were mostly rock and roll and southern rock; and their edgier performances.

Bo Bice would end up making it all the way to the finals, competing head-to-head against Carrie Underwood for the 2005 *American Idol* title. Both Underwood and Bice would become fan favorites throughout Season Four.

Reawakening the Dream

It was during the fall of 2004, when Underwood was about to begin her senior year of college, that auditions for the fourth season of *American Idol* were under way. Underwood was doing well in college and was looking forward to graduating the following spring. She was active in a number of clubs and had mostly put aside any interest in pursuing a professional singing career. "After high school, I pretty much gave up on my dream of singing," Underwood wrote on her Web site. "I had reached a point in my life where I had to be practical and prepare for my future in the real world."

Meanwhile, the *American Idol* auditions were taking place, and the attention from the media was great. There were constant news reports about the number of people auditioning at the various sites around the country. One night, while home from college to visit her family, Underwood caught a news broadcast and was inspired. "I was at home one weekend and saw on the news that many people were in Cleveland, Ohio, sleeping outside in hopes of auditioning for the 2005 season of *American Idol*," Underwood wrote on her Web site. "People always told me I should try out for the show, but I never thought I could handle it." But her family and friends thought differently. They urged her to audition.

Underwood was soon researching information on where auditions would be taking place and if she met the audition criteria. St. Louis, Missouri, was the closest audition site to her hometown, yet the city was still several hours away by car. Something about that newscast stayed with Underwood, however, and she frequently thought about going to the audition. "One day, I thought, 'I'm going to graduate and I don't know what I'm going to do, so why not try out for *American Idol*? What's the worst that could happen? If I don't make it past the audition, nobody's going to know,'" she told *Reader's Digest*. Underwood would make it past the audition and beyond, and soon the whole country would know about her.

The St. Louis Audition

One night, after she finished performing at a college show, Underwood's mom drove her, her friend, and her friend's mother to the auditions in St. Louis. They drove through the night and arrived at 6:00 AM the next morning. Underwood waited in line with thousands of other singers, all of them hoping they would have a chance to audition.

Underwood accepts the award for Album of the Year at the Academy of Country Music Awards from her favorite country singer, Martina McBride.

After waiting for more than eight hours, Underwood was asked to sing in front of one of the show's producers. She sang a song by Martina McBride, her favorite country music singer. The song was called "Phones Are Ringing All Over the Town." When she finished singing for the producer, Underwood was disappointed by her performance. She didn't think she had done very well. But to her surprise, she was invited back the next day to sing for one of the show's executive producers. The next day Underwood sang another McBride song called "Independence Day." Again, she made it to the next round.

Underwood was now in the final and most important round of auditions, and this time it was different. Instead of performing in front of another *American Idol* producer, she would be singing in front of the show's three judges: Randy Jackson, a record producer and Grammy Award–winning bass player; Paula Abdul, a former multiplatinum-selling pop singer; and Simon Cowell, a music executive and a judge on a number of television talent shows, including *Britain's Pop Idol, The X Factor,* and *Britain's Got Talent.*

This performance, in front of the famous trio of judges, was the most important of the auditions. If she did well, Underwood would be invited to Hollywood to appear on the show and compete against other semifinalists for a record contract. If she didn't do well, she would be going home, perhaps with one of Cowell's patented withering put-downs ringing in her ears.

For this audition, Underwood sang a song called "I Can't Make You Love Me," by singer-songwriter Bonnie Raitt. Her innocent charm and pure, pretty voice captured the attention of the judges, and they invited her to Hollywood to be on the show.

Season Four's auditions would see the biggest crowds to date for the show, with more than 21,000 hopefuls attending the Washington, D.C., audition alone. The auditions also drew celebrity guests. Pop singer Brandy and Gene Simmons, bass player and vocalist of the rock band Kiss, participated in the audition process and gave their critique of performances.

American Idol's judges, Randy Jackson, Paula Abdul, and Simon Cowell, sit front and center during the singing competition, ready to critique performances and provide advice.

Going to Hollywood

Underwood's trip to Hollywood, California, the capital of the American film and television industry, was her very first plane ride. In the car, while she drove with her parents to the airport, Underwood began to cry as her fear of flying consumed her. "On the way to the airport, my mom stopped at the store. I started to cry in the car with my dad," Underwood told *Reader's Digest*. "I said, 'I don't want to fly.' And he said, 'Well, we can turn around right now and go back home if you want.' I thought how something silly like not wanting to get on a plane might keep me from doing something cool." Underwood faced her fears head-on, got on the plane, and made it safely to Hollywood.

In January 2005, the fourth season of *American Idol* began airing on television. Each year, before the competition and voting portions of the show begin, *American Idol* airs episodes that show highlights and lowlights drawn from the nationwide auditions. These early episodes show viewers what it's like to audition for the show and where the auditions take place. They also show each audition site's best and worst performances, one of the most popular parts of each season's broadcasts.

Underwood's final audition was featured in one of these early episodes. When it aired on television, many people predicted right off the bat that she would win the competition.

Chapter 3

WINNING IT ALL

The fourth season of *American Idol* premiered on January 18, 2005. This year would prove to be a showdown between country music and rock 'n' roll. Carrie Underwood, who mostly performed songs by country artists, competed against singers who showed their range with songs that had been made famous by pop artists and rock 'n' roll bands.

The fourth season also saw a change in how the competition would be structured. In the past, contestants competed in semifinal rounds, and the singers with the most votes were promoted to the final round. This year, twenty-four semifinalists were named: twelve men and twelve women. Instead of competing against the entire group, contestants competed separately, with two women and two men voted off the show each week by the judges. This continued until just the top twelve finalists were left. The top twelve

The final twelve contestants of Season Four of *American Idol*: *(bottom row, left to right)* Carrie Underwood, Mario Vazquez, Mikalah Gordon, and Jessica Sierra; *(back row, left to right)* Constantine Maroulis, Nadia Turner, Bo Bice, Vonzell Solomon, Anthony Fedorov, Lindsey Cardinale, Anwar Robinson, and Scott Savol.

then began to compete against each other for the public's call-in votes.

Making the Cut

Underwood's first semifinal performance was the song "Could've Been," by the eighties-era pop singer Tiffany. Underwood performed the song so well that judge Randy Jackson told her he couldn't believe that no one had discovered her yet.

Easily making it into the top twelve, Underwood chose songs for the semifinal round that showed her diverse range as a singer. She performed "Piece of My Heart," by sixties-era rock singer Janis Joplin, and the ballad "Because You Loved Me," by the contemporary pop singer Celine Dion. Even though Underwood moved very easily between the different styles of songs she performed on the show, she was always nervous when she performed. "Knowing that 30 million people are watching you, that one of the judges could tell you you're horrible, or you could forget the words or mess up . . . it was a lot of pressure," Underwood told *Self* magazine.

There were many nights when Underwood just wanted to leave it all behind and go home. But she persisted for fear that she might be giving up her last chance of making it as a singer. "I just knew that if I didn't try, and if I didn't handle things the best I could, and if I didn't do my best all the time, then I couldn't think, 'What if?' for the rest of my life," Underwood said in the *Self* interview.

A Little Bit Country, A Little Bit Rock 'n' Roll

As the show continued each week, two contestants emerged as popular standouts, Underwood and Bo Bice. Bice was a native of Huntsville, Alabama. He became well known for his deep, baritone voice and for his unique style of incorporating soul, blues, and rock into his performances. When Bice performed "Whipping Post" by the Allman Brothers Band, he drew rave reviews from the judges and established himself as a fan favorite among *American Idol* viewers.

Underwood gave *American Idol* audiences their first real taste of country music, after three years of the show being dominated by pop and R & B music. With consistent performances and a genuine down-to-earth kindness, Underwood became something of an audience sweetheart.

Though she sang a wide range of songs in a number of different styles on the show, Underwood preferred to perform

Underwood performs with country group Rascal Flatts during the *American Idol* finale. Later that night, Underwood was crowned the winner.

With a Song in Her Heart

Carrie Underwood's list of songs performed on *American Idol*:

WEEK	SONG	ORIGINAL ARTIST
Semifinals 1	"Could've Been"	Tiffany
Semifinals 2	"Piece of My Heart"	Janis Joplin
Semifinals 3	"Because You Loved Me"	Celine Dion
Top 12	"When Will I Be Loved?"	Linda Ronstadt
Top 11	"Alone"	Heart
Top 10	"Independence Day"	Martina McBride
Top 9	"Hello, Young Lovers"	Deborah Kerr
Top 8	"Love Is a Battlefield"	Pat Benatar
Top 7	"MacArthur Park"	Donna Summer
Top 6	"When God-Fearin' Women Get the Blues"	Martina McBride
Top 5	"Trouble," "Bless the Broken Road"	Elvis Presley, Rascal Flatts
Top 4	"If You Don't Know Me by Now," "Sin Wagon"	Harold Melvin & the Blue Notes, Dixie Chicks
Top 3	"Crying," "Man! I Feel Like a Woman!," "Making Love Out of Nothing at All"	Roy Orbison, Shania Twain, Air Supply
Top 2	"Inside Your Heaven," "Independence Day," "Angels Brought Me Here"	Carrie Underwood, Martina McBride, Guy Sebastian
Final song of *American Idol* Season Four	"Inside Your Heaven"	Carrie Underwood

songs associated with country singers. Many of her choices were by some of country music's biggest artists, including Rascal Flatts, the Dixie Chicks, Martina McBride, and Shania Twain. Bice preferred songs by southern rock bands such as the Allman Brothers Band and Lynyrd Skynyrd.

Simon Predicts a Winner

On the March 22, 2005, *American Idol* episode, after a performance of "Alone," a song written and made famous by the rock band Heart, Underwood waited on stage for the judges to comment on her performance. Simon Cowell, the *Idol* judge famous for being hard to please and nasty in his comments, told Underwood, "You're not just the girl to beat, you're the person to beat. I will make a prediction: not only will you win this competition, but you will sell more records than any other previous *Idol* winner."

The following week, on the March 30 show, Underwood performed the song "Independence Day" by country singer Martina McBride, the same song she performed during her auditions. After her performance, Cowell commented that Underwood had the "It" factor that would make her a star.

Underwood advanced in the competition, watching each week as her fellow contestants were voted off. After entering the top three, Underwood and the two remaining contestants, Bo Bice and Vonzell Solomon, were each flown back to their hometowns. Underwood returned to Checotah, Oklahoma, and was greeted by more than 10,000 people, all welcoming the singer home with a parade led by her high school's marching band. Underwood performed the national anthem for her hometown, which had supported her throughout her appearance on *American Idol*.

Underwood returned to Hollywood and made it to the final round of *American Idol*, where she would square off against Bo Bice. On the night of the final performance, Underwood and Bice each performed three songs. Underwood sang "Inside Your Heaven" (a song written especially for the final two *American Idol* contestants by Andreas Carlsson, Pelle Nylén, and Savan Kotecha), "Independence Day," and "Angels Brought Me Here," a song by Guy Sebastian.

Underwood's performance of "Angels Brought Me Here" was outstanding and inspired Cowell to comment to Underwood and the entire television audience, "I think you've done enough to win the competition." Judge Randy Jackson gave Underwood his first and only standing ovation of the season.

Winning *American Idol* and Going Country

More than thirty-seven million people voted for the Season Four winner of *American Idol*. A fan favorite from the beginning, Underwood was named the winner on May 25, 2005. She became only the second winner never to be voted in the bottom three during any point in the show's season. She also never faced elimination.

As part of her winnings, Underwood received a $1 million record deal with Arista Records Nashville, whose artists include

And the American Idol is . . . Carrie Underwood is named the winner of *American Idol* by show host Ryan Seacrest as fellow finalist Bo Bice looks on.

Brooks and Dunn, Alan Jackson, and Brad Paisley—all top country music performers. She also signed a contract with 19 Management, an artist management company founded by *American Idol*-creator Simon Fuller.

Shortly after being named the winner of *American Idol*, Underwood decided to stick with country music instead of choosing to perform pop music like a number of *American Idol* winners before her. She is the only *American Idol* winner to record and perform country music exclusively.

Chapter 4

HITTING THE AIRWAVES

When Carrie Underwood won *American Idol*, she immediately became a frequent guest on talk shows and the subject of interviews—all to talk about her *American Idol* experience. She was ushered off to photo shoots for magazines, and, most important to her, to a recording studio to work on her debut album.

While she worked with songwriters on new music and gathered material for her first album, the single "Inside Your Heaven" was released to radio, and it became an instant hit due to the fan base *American Idol* had created for her.

A Hit and a Record Contract

With fans of *American Idol* already familiar with "Inside Your Heaven," the song debuted in the number 1 spot on

The night after she won *American Idol*, Underwood began a publicity tour. In the above photo, she stops by the *Tonight Show with Jay Leno* for an interview.

the Billboard Top 100 and the Canadian Singles charts, selling more than 170,000 copies in its first week. The song was eventually certified gold by the Recording Industry Association of America (RIAA) and two times platinum by the Canadian Recording Industry Association (CRIA). While the song was very popular and ended up being the top-selling song of the year in the Billboard charts, it was shunned by the country music industry for being too pop. It received very little country radio airplay and, as a result, reached only number 53 on the country music charts. But this was hardly a setback for Underwood.

After releasing "Inside your Heaven," Underwood immediately began selecting songs for her debut album, which she titled *Some Hearts*. The album's selections seemed to represent Underwood's personal journey from small-town girl to the glitter and glamour of superstardom. The album's songs, she said, allowed her to draw on different aspects of her personality. "Happy songs, sad songs, and angry songs—it's cool to have a lot of contrast," Underwood said in describing her album to PopMatters.com. "It's fun to play all those roles."

The album's first release, "Jesus, Take the Wheel," was the first song Underwood felt a strong connection to. "It's such a great story," she said in an interview with *SingerUniverse* magazine. "The song tells such a great story. Fortunately, everyone around me felt the same way about the song as I did, so recording it and making it my first single was really a no-brainer."

A Series of Number 1 Hits

"Jesus, Take the Wheel" hit the airways on October 18, 2005, and was played constantly on country radio stations. Because of this intense airplay, the song debuted at number 39 on the Billboard Country Chart, setting a record. It became the first single from a new artist's debut album to hold the number 1 spot for six consecutive weeks.

On November 15, 2005, Underwood's album, *Some Hearts*, was released in stores. In its first week, the album sold more than 314,000 copies, making it the highest-selling debut album by a country artist. The album debuted in the number 1 spot and came in at number 2 on the Billboard 200. Underwood immediately promoted the album with appearances on *The Tonight Show with Jay Leno, The Today Show*, and *The View*.

Following the success of "Jesus, Take the Wheel," Underwood released her next single, "Don't Forget to Remember Me." This particular song held a special place in her heart. When Underwood first heard the song, she cried. She was homesick at the time and missed her family. The song tells the story of a young girl leaving home for the first time. It made Underwood think of her own journey leaving home and living on her own. She accidentally sent the lyrics to the song along with some paperwork home to her parents. Her mother, Carole, received the package in the mail, read through the lyrics, and called her. "This is our song," her mother told her. "In that moment," Underwood wrote on her Web site, "I knew that no matter how hard it was to get through, I had to record it." "Don't Forget to Remember Me" became Underwood's second number 1 hit.

With her debut album, *Some Hearts*, hitting stores, Underwood performs on the *Today Show* in November 2005.

And the Winner Is . . .

A list of awards Underwood has received since winning the 2005 *American Idol* contest:

2005 • Teen Choice Awards, Choice Reality Star—Female
   • Billboard Music Awards, Top-Selling Hot 100 Song of the Year: "Inside Your Heaven"
   • Billboard Music Awards, Top-Selling Country Single: "Inside Your Heaven"
   • Billboard Music Awards, Country Single Sales Artist of the Year

2006 • Gospel Music Association Awards, Country Recorded Song of the Year: "Jesus, Take the Wheel"
   • Country Music Television (CMT) Music Awards, Female Video of the Year: "Jesus, Take the Wheel"
   • CMT Music Awards, Breakthrough Video of the Year: "Jesus, Take the Wheel"
   • Academy of Country Music Awards, Top New Female Vocalist of the Year
   • Academy of Country Music Awards, Single Record of the Year: "Jesus, Take the Wheel"
   • Music Row Award, Critics Pick
   • Country Music Association Awards, Female Vocalist of the Year
   • Country Music Association Awards, Horizon Award
   • 12th Annual Inspirational Country Music Awards, Mainstream Country Artist of the Year
   • American Music Awards, Favorite New Breakthrough Artist
   • Billboard Music Awards, Female Country Artist of the Year
   • Billboard Music Awards, Album of the Year: *Some Hearts*
   • Billboard Music Awards, Country Album of the Year: *Some Hearts*
   • Billboard Music Awards, Country New Artist of the Year
   • Billboard Music Awards, Female Billboard 200 Album Artist of the Year

2007 • People's Choice Awards, Favorite Country Song: "Before He Cheats"
   • People's Choice Awards, Favorite Female Singer

- Grammy Awards, Best New Artist
- Grammy Awards, Best Female Country Vocal Performance: "Jesus, Take the Wheel"
- Grammy Awards, Best Country Song: "Jesus, Take the Wheel"
- CMT Music Awards, Video of the Year: "Before He Cheats"
- CMT Music Awards, Female Video of the Year: "Before He Cheats"
- Academy of Country Music Awards, Top Female Vocalist
- Academy of Country Music Awards, Album of the Year: *Some Hearts*
- Academy of Country Music Awards, Video of the Year: "Before He Cheats"

Underwood's third single was a significant departure from the songs she had released to date. It also raised some eyebrows and caused a bit of a stir. "Before He Cheats," the story of an angry girlfriend who discovers her boyfriend's cheating ways, was a mix of country and rock. The lyrics describe actions that seem to contradict Underwood's wholesome, all-American sweetheart image. The potential controversy prompted Underwood to make a disclaimer on her Web site: "I decided to sing ("Before He Cheats") because I think that everyone has a 'mean streak,' and the character in the song has a very large one. I would like to say, however, that I do not condone the destruction of anyone's property and I have never, at any time, keyed anyone's car."

"Before He Cheats" became Underwood's third number 1 single, landing on the Hot Country Songs chart for five consecutive weeks. It also peaked at number 8 on the Hot 100 chart, making it a huge crossover hit for Underwood. In fact, the song was the biggest hit from her *Some Hearts* album.

The fourth single released from *Some Hearts* was "Wasted." The song also debuted at number 1 on the country charts and marked a fourth number 1 hit for Underwood. *Some Hearts* would turn out to be the most successful debut album by any *American Idol* winner. In total, the album stayed on Billboard's Top Country Albums chart for more than twenty weeks, more than any other country album in 2005. The album also has the distinction of being the best-selling single disc album by a solo country artist in the last six years. *Some Hearts* has been certified platinum six times, having sold more than six million copies.

Honors and Endorsements

Following the release of *Some Hearts*, Underwood began receiving nominations for a number of awards honoring her music and performances. Since her *American Idol* win, Underwood has won more than twenty-nine different awards. Among her honors are three Grammy Awards.

The Grammys are the music industry's most prestigious honors. Presented by the National Academy of Recording Arts and Sciences, the Grammy Awards honor artistic achievement, technical proficiency, and overall excellence in the recording industry. Underwood won the coveted Best New Artist award and was honored with two awards for her single "Jesus, Take the Wheel." The song won the awards for Best Female

Vocal Performance and Best Country Song. Underwood has also been honored by the country music industry, winning a number of awards from the Academy of Country Music, country music's most prominent honors.

In addition to awards for her music, Underwood has landed lucrative product endorsement deals, doing print advertisements and television commercials for everything from Hershey's chocolate to SKECHERS sneakers.

While she has traveled around the world, performed

Underwood poses with her two Grammys backstage in 2007. She won for Best New Artist and Best Female Country Vocal Performance.

in front of millions of fans on tour, and received some of the music industry's highest honors, Underwood is still a small-town girl at heart. She just happened to make it big singing the music that she loved listening to growing up. "I have known all my life that being a country music singer would be the most wonderful thing that I could ever do," she told *SingerUniverse* magazine. "I am so grateful for this opportunity, and I want more than anything for my family, friends, and fans to be proud of me and the music that I make."

Glossary

Billboard Hot Country Songs A list of the most popular country songs, calculated weekly by airplay and commercial sales.

Billboard Top 100 A list of the 100 best-selling albums in America.

Billboard 200 A list of the 200 best-selling albums in America.

Canadian Recording Industry Association (CRIA) A nonprofit organization that was founded in 1964 to represent the interests of Canadian companies that create, manufacture, and market sound recordings.

Country Music Association (CMA) An organization of country music industry professionals that guides and enhances the development of country music throughout the world and demonstrates that country music is a viable and popular medium to advertisers, consumers, and media. The association annually hosts the CMA Awards.

crossover hit A song that originates in one musical genre (for example, R & B) and becomes popular in a second, different genre (such as country), or a song that appeals to various types of audiences, such as rap fans and rock 'n' roll listeners.

CTV Canada's preeminent broadcast communications company. CTV features conventional television operations across Canada and is a leader in providing specialty television to Canadian viewers.

Grammy Awards The Grammy Awards are the only peer-presented awards to honor artistic achievement, technical proficiency, and overall excellence in the recording industry. They are awarded by the National Academy of Recording Arts and Sciences.

Music Row Located in Nashville, Tennessee, Music Row was developed in the 1950s as a headquarters and creative center of the country music recording industry.

Music Row Critics Pick Award An award that honors an outstanding new artist who has released his or her first single in the past year.

Recording Industry Association of America (RIAA) The trade group that represents the U.S. recording industry.

For More Information

Academy of Country Music
5500 Balboa Boulevard, Suite 200
Encino, CA 91316
(818) 788-8000
Web site: http://www.acmcountry.com
 The Academy of Country Music (ACM) was founded in 1964 in Los Angeles,
 California, and initially sought to promote country music in the western
 states. Today, it hosts the annual Academy of Country Music Awards
 ceremony.

Canadian Country Music Association
626 King Street West, Suite 203
Toronto, ON M5V 1M7
Canada
(416) 947-1331
Web site: http://www.ccma.org
 The Canadian Country Music Association (CCMA) is a nonprofit professional trade organization whose purpose is to protect the heritage of,
 advocate the development of, and enact laws favorable to the Canadian
 country music industry domestically and internationally. Since 1976, the
 CCMA has been committed to ensuring the growth of the Canadian
 country music industry.

Country Music Hall of Fame and Museum
222 Fifth Avenue South
Nashville, TN 37203
(615) 416-2001

Web site: http://www.countrymusichalloffame.com/site
   The Country Music Hall of Fame and Museum is operated by the nonprofit,
   educational Country Music Foundation (CMF). The mission of the CMF is
   to identify and preserve the evolving history and traditions of country music
   and to educate its audiences.

Country Music Television
330 Commerce Street
Nashville, TN 37201
(615) 335-8400
Web site: http://www.cmt.com
   A cable television channel devoted exclusively to country music
   programming.

Country Weekly Magazine
118 16th Avenue South, Suite 230
Nashville, TN 37203
Web site: http://www.countryweekly.com
   A magazine devoted to country music, artists, and industry news.

Web Sites

Due to the changing nature of Internet links, Rosen Publishing
has developed an online list of Web sites related to the subject
of this book. This site is updated regularly. Please use this link to
access the list:

http://www.rosenlinks.com/wyi/caun

For Further Reading

Austen, Jake. *TV-a-Go-Go: Rock on TV from American Bandstand to American Idol.* Chicago, IL: Chicago Review Press, 2005.

Baskerville, David. *Music Business Handbook and Career Guide.* Thousand Oaks, CA: Sage Publications, Inc., 2005.

Britten, Anna. *Working in the Music Industry: How to Find an Exciting and Varied Career in the World of Music.* Oxford, England: How To Books, 2006.

Cowell, Simon. *I Don't Mean to Be Rude, But . . . : Backstage Gossip from American Idol & the Secrets That Can Make You a Star.* New York, NY: Broadway Books, 2003.

Field, Shelly. *Career Opportunities in the Music Industry.* New York, NY: Checkmark Books, 2004.

McDowell, Josh. *American Idols: The Worship of the American Dream.* Nashville, TN: B & H Publishing, 2006.

Rich, Jason. *American Idol Season 4: Behind-the-Scenes Fan Book.* Roseville, CA: Prima Games, 2005.

Tracy, Kathleen. *Carrie Underwood.* Hockessin, DE: Mitchell Lane Publishers, 2005.

Walsh, Marissa. *American Idol: The Search for a Superstar—The Official Book.* New York, NY: Bantam Books for Young Readers, 2002.

Bibliography

Access Hollywood. "Carrie Underwood Graduates College." 2006. Retrieved May 7, 2007 (http://www.accesshollywood.com/news/ah181.shtml).

Associated Press. "Carrie Underwood Has Her Town Talking." MSNBC. May 9, 2005. Retrieved June 29, 2007 (http://www.msnbc.msn.com/id/7794328).

CMT. "Carrie Underwood." Retrieved April 12, 2007 (http://www.cmt.com/artists/az/underwood_carrie/bio.jhtml).

CMT. "Carrie Underwood's Debut CD Pounces into Top Album Spot." November 26, 2005. Retrieved April 19, 2007 (http://www.cmt.com/news/articles/1514481/20051123/underwood__carrie.jhtml?headlines=true).

CNN.com. "Chesney Wins Country Entertainer of the Year." May 16, 2007. Retrieved May 16, 2007 (http://www.cnn.com/2007/SHOWBIZ/Music/05/16.country.awards.ap/index.html).

Dehnart, Andy. "'Idol' Season Four: Country vs. Rock and Roll." MSNBC. January 20, 2006. Retrieved July 10, 2007 (http://www.msnbc.msn.com/id/10456158).

Ford, Tracey. "Carrie Tops Bo as Idol." May 26, 2005. Rolling Stone. Retrieved April 12, 2007 (http://www.rollingstone.com/artists/americanidol/articles/story/7359874/carrie_tops_bo_as_idol).

Gardner, Tom. "Chesney, Underwood Win Country Awards." USA TODAY. May 15, 2007. Retrieved May 16, 2007 (http://www.usatoday.com/life/music/news/2007-05-15-country-music-awards_N.htm).

Kaplan, James. "How American Idol's Carrie Underwood Went from Small-Town Girl to Big-Time Star." Parade, October 22, 2006, pp. 4–5.

Kidzworld.com. "Casting Call—*American Idol 4.*" Retrieved
　　July 10, 2007 (http://www.kidzworld.com/article/4619-casting-
　　call-american-idol-4).

Kingsbury, Paul, ed. *The Encyclopedia of Country Music: The Ultimate
　　Guide to the Music.* New York, NY: Oxford University Press, 2004.

Nash, Alanna. "America's Idol." *Reader's Digest,* June 2006. Retrieved
　　April 18, 2007 (http://www.rd.com/content/printContent.do?
　　contentId=26895).

Rentmeester, Coliena, and Mark Abrahams. "*Self* Chats with *American
　　Idol* Carrie Underwood." *Self.* Retrieved April 12, 2007 (http://
　　www.self.com/livingwell/articles/2006/03/20/0321carrie).

Rich, Jason. *American Idol Season 4: Behind-the-Scenes Fan Book.*
　　Roseville, CA: Prima Games, 2005.

Sindy. "Carrie Underwood Interview." Kidzworld.com. Retrieved July 9,
　　2007 (http://www.kidzworld.com/article/6222-carrie-underwood-
　　interview).

Tracy, Kathleen. *Carrie Underwood.* Hockessin, DE: Mitchell Lane
　　Publishers, 2005.

Tranter, Nikki. "Superstar Tourism: An Interview with Carrie Underwood."
　　PopMatters.com. February 8, 2006. Retrieved May 7, 2007 (http://
　　www.popmatters.com/music/interviews/underwood-carrie-
　　060208.shtml).

Walsh, Marissa. *American Idol: The Search for a Superstar—The Official
　　Book.* New York, NY: Bantam Books for Young Readers, 2002.

Index

About the Author

Laura La Bella works full-time as a writer and editor at Rochester Institute of Technology. She lives in Rochester, New York, with her husband, a social studies teacher, and their two cats.

Photo Credits

Designer: Tahara Anderson; **Photo Researcher:** Amy Feinberg